Hannah

To two wom[en] ———— —
a reminder of your life
in beautiful California!
I miss you!
Merry Christmas!
Love Jen

Northern
CALIFORNIA

Northern CALIFORNIA

Larry Ulrich & Willard Clay

with an introduction by
Sandra L. Keith

SKYLINE PRESS

Acknowledgements

Our thanks are due to many friends who have helped
in the work on this book and especially to
ARMANDO QUINTERO and JEAN JONES

Produced by Boulton Publishing Services, Inc., Toronto
Designed by Fortunato Aglialoro

©1986 Oxford University Press (Canadian Branch)
SKYLINE PRESS is a registered imprint of the Oxford University Press

ISBN 0-19-540635-4
1 2 3 4-9 8 7 6

Color separation by LASERSHARP Inc., Toronto

Printed in Hong Kong by Scanner Art Services Inc., Toronto

INTRODUCTION

Say the words, 'Northern California', to anyone familiar with the Golden State's upper half and you'll evoke a hundred different images. To some, Northern California is sparkling rivers and streams, fog-moody estuaries, and a wave-chewed coastline. To others, the words conjure up pictures of the Napa and Sonoma Valleys' far-reaching vineyards, the rusted relics of the Mother Lode's mining heyday, and the volcanic conflagration of the Cascadian peaks called Shasta and Lassen. Still others think only of the magnificent Sierra Nevada, that land of serrated crests, suicidal waterfalls, and glacially-polished granite that glistens like glass.

To me, long-time resident of the state's semi-arid southern reaches, Northern California is synonymous with the coast redwoods, those massive auburn colonnades whose mesmerizing beauty lies not so much in individual specimens as in the forest as a whole. They are cloudsweeping monarchs, once covering more than two million acres of coastline, from Big Sur on the south to Oregon's Chetco River on the north. And even though most of the giant trees have been reduced to lumber and scattered across the world in every form imaginable, those remaining constitute a forest that once seen is remembered forever.

To give the impression that all of Northern California is naught but a huge and lovely wilderness would be greatly unfair. Of course there are areas where towns stand shoulder to shoulder and jungles of neon light up the night. Even the pastoral communities are often joined edge to edge as dairy farms and hayfields crazy-quilt a thousand rolling hills; orchards spread across valley floors and up the sides of mountains; and an army of vegetables casts leafy blankets across the arable flatlands.

Yet even those places where civilization twists back on itself seem of no consequence when stacked against the abundance of Northern California's mind-boggling landscapes. For what is cosmopolitan San Francisco compared to the lonely, windswept headlands of Point Reyes or the azure finger of Tomales Bay or the millenniums-old redwoods of Muir Woods? And how can Sacramento, the state capital, compete with the pristine scenery of the Feather River Canyon? Or the springtime flower-explosion in the Sierran foothills? Or the lazy waterways of the Sacramento-San Joaquin Delta, with its nearly 700 miles of meandering channels?

Such are the entities that make the state's northern sector so appealing. And nowhere is the appeal stronger or the magnetism greater than in the Sierra Nevada—the highest and longest unbroken mountain range in the lower 48 states. In its entirety, the range is a 400-mile-long granite block, thrust from the bowels of the earth, glaciated into a tangle of sawteeth, and dissected further by eons of wind and rain and snow and ice. The imposing mass varies in width from 50 to 80 miles and presents such a formidable barrier that even today only five roads cross its wilds—and four of those are snowbound from November until May or June.

Yet for all its austerity, the range is a horde of primeval beauty. The Indians claimed it was *Inyo*, "dwelling place of a great spirit." Early Spanish explorers named it *una gran sierra nevada*, "a great snowy range." Noted conservationist John Muir observed that the sun shining on wave after wave of glacially polished rock caused the mountains to appear lit from within and dubbed them poetically, "the range of light." Geologically, it is simply the Sierra Nevada.

Despite a relative inaccessibility and short visitation season, it seems that at one time or another all humanity enters the Sierra's rugged portals. The reasons are multiple: Reno, San Francisco, and Sacramento are all within easy distance, all are popular destinations, and all offer main thoroughways into the Sierran wilderness. Yet perhaps more than anything else, it is a nebulous something called the Sierran Mystique that draws visitors from all across the continent and half a world away. For this land of wind-crusted snow, mini-glaciers, boulder-strewn alpine meadows, and stark, granite deserts has a charm all its own. And whether the ambiance is wind-borne or spring-fed or wafts upward from the very marrow of the range itself, one fact is certain: it is there.

Rich is the one who takes time to savor the aura. Most of the untamed high country lies within the protective embrace of three national parks, one national monument, nine national forests, and multiple primitive and wilderness areas. Within those confines are the world-renowned Yosemite Valley; the giant sequoias of Yosemite, Sequoia, and Kings Canyon; the basaltic columns called Devil's Postpile; the turquoise expanse of Lake Tahoe, one of North America's deepest waterways; the spectacular 4,000- to 8,000-foot-deep Kings Canyon; and the 14,495-foot-high Mount Whitney—highest peak in the contiguous states.

Spectacular as it is, the high Sierra scenery is not solely responsible for the range's charm. Sprinkled throughout the foothills are the ghostly reminders of California's burnished past, and they have names like Mariposa, Chinese Camp, Coloma, Dry-town, Grass Valley, Mokelumne Hill, Columbia, and Downieville.

The Sierran boomtowns changed the course of American history, creating a new frontier that was ever on the move and populated by many-hued adventurers whose roots went down only as far as the hills' high-grade ore. It was a time when shanty towns grew up almost overnight and disappeared nearly as fast; where noise, clatter, mud, dirt, stones, and water accompanied ragged clothes, big boots, picks, and shovels; where the only ones who really struck it rich were those who supplied the tools of the trade; where glorious images of wealth were quickly replaced by burnt-out hope.

Mexican miners named the incredibly rich gold vein that stretched 120 miles from Bear Valley to Auburn, *La Veta Madre*, "The Mother Lode." The name gradually came to describe the entire foothill region. By any title, the Gold Rush of 1849 was one of the most frantic migrations in human history, and although many of the boomtowns are now nothing more than names recorded in the annals of yesteryear, much remains—especially along the 325-mile length of highway called, appropriately, State 49.

It is a timewarp into the past. Some of the towns have been restored and are now state historic parks. A few have kept pace, becoming modern versions of their former selves. But most are a hodgepodge of ruined walls whose sole support comes from the sturdiness of their iron doors and shutters. Countless more are naught but toe-stubbing rubble hidden amidst ever-encroaching vegetation. Yet no matter what their present condition, all claim a common denominator: they are silent testimonies to the time when the Golden State exploded.

Just north of the Sierra Nevada lies one of California's best-kept secrets—a diverse and wildly fascinating realm that, even in this populous state, remains largely undiscovered. It is a region dominated by three large mountain ranges: the Klamath-Scott, which includes the Trinity, Shasta, and Marble Mountains; the Warner Mountains, an isolated spur of the Cascades; and the southernmost reaches of the Cascades themselves, a spectacular string of volcanic sentinels that begins in British Columbia and ends in Northern California.

In its entirety, the area stretches from the upper Sacramento Valley north to Oregon, west to the Coast Range, and east to Nevada. Travel brochures often refer to this somewhat pie-shaped region as Lake Country, an apt title for the home of the Klamath, Trinity, Salmon, and Sacramento rivers as well as a host of recreational lakes named Eagle, Shasta, Almanor, Siskiyou, Whiskeytown, and Clair Engle. But to Californians it is simply the Northern Mountains—a place where the vestiges of a volcanic past hopscotch an emerald wilderness.

Nowhere else in the state is there such a capricious collection of landforms. Within a few miles of one another are steep, mountainous uplands and stark cinder cones, glacial tarns and blurping mud-pots, alpine highlands and pumice plains, wildlife refuges and steaming hot springs, white-spumed waterfalls and black-glass cliffs, serene lakes and hissing fumaroles, pine-scented breezes and eye-stinging sulphuric clouds. It is a world both weird and wonderful. And at its heart stands Mount Shasta, the double-coned volcano whose snow-mantled crest looms over the Northland like a white-robed colossus.

On a clear day you can see it 100 miles away. Remote. Ethereal. Its icy peak stands 14,162 feet high; its diameter spans 17 miles; its 4.7 billion cubic feet of ice constitutes five separate glaciers whose meltwaters give rise to the Shasta, McCloud, and Sacramento Rivers. It is a great, freestanding monarch created not by one cataclysmic event, but by eons of successive volcanic activity interrupted by long periods of quiet. It is quiet now. So quiet in fact that many claim Mount Shasta is either dead or dying. But not so. Like its Cascade counterparts (St. Helens excepted), Shasta only slumbers. And even though the mountain's pyroclastic displays claim no place in historical records, its carbon-blue shoulders wear the tortuous scars of lava flows a scant 300 years old.

The volcanic debris on Lassen is younger still. The 10,457-foot-high peak is one of the world's largest plug-dome volcanoes, and until Mount St. Helens began its infamous escapades in 1980, Lassen was the most fretful mountain in the contiguous states. Its last eruptive cycle began in 1914 and ended in 1921, although steam clouds at the summit were visible into the early 1940s. It mattered not that the cratered peak slept beneath a cap of winter white; the volcanic innards still boiled. It is so today. And nowhere is Lassen's fiery tumult more evident than at the hydrothermal areas called Sulphur Works, Devil's Kitchen, Boiling Springs Lake, and Bumpass Hell—a mile-wide valley discovered and named by Kendall Bumpass, who fatally burned a leg when he accidentally stepped into one of the area's steaming pools.

Tucked midway between Lassen and Shasta is Burney Falls, a 129-foot-high twin waterfall which so impressed President Theodore Roosevelt that he called it the "eighth wonder of the world." Sprawling toward the northeast, into what was once Modoc Indian country, is the inhospitable jumble of the Burnt Lava Flow, the sapphire circle that is Medicine Lake, a jet-black mass of obsidion called Glass Mountain, and a necklace of lakes that have long been national wildlife refuges.

Here, too, is Lava Beds National Monument, an incoherent collection of igneous rock, spatter cones, craters, and lava tubes—some of which are a mile and a half long, and most of which provided the Modoc Indians and their chief, Captain Jack, with strongholds so unbreachable it took the U.S. Cavalry nearly six months to win what turned out to be California's only major Indian war.

While the Northern Mountains rank as one of the states' least publicized regions, the North Coast is known far and wide as a tantalizing mecca set against the broad expanse of the Pacific. It is a place where towns are few, unspoiled vistas are many, and dairy cows outnumber humans by unimaginable numbers. The terrain is mountainous—dissected by canyons, cut through by rivers and streams, freckled by oak woodlands, swatched by coniferous forests, battle-stung by the ocean's unending assaults, and stalked by a gray gauze mist that plays cat-and-mouse with headlands and treetops alike.

And that is only the windshield scene. Those willing to leave the asphalt discover unexpected treasures—tidepools filled with an array of creatures whose whole lives are an in-again, out-again existence. Tidal souvenirs decorating everything from sandy pocket beaches to rocky shoals. Wave-pounded islets where California sea lions snooze in the sun. Ocean-washed mud flats whose early morning tracery reads like a hotel register for critters. Marshes patrolled by egrets and herons. Brown pelicans skimming supper from the sea, clouds of sea gulls following fishing boats, and bewhiskered harbor seals openly spying on human beachwalkers.

There is, of course, no actual signpost or definitive landmark that announces where this magnificent wonderland begins, and Californians are often at odds as to where the invisible border lies. Some claim everything from Santa Barbara to Oregon is exclusively the North Coast. Others believe Monterey is the jumping-off spot. More than a few acknowledge San Francisco as the one true gateway. Whatever the preconceived notions, map-makers note the Golden State's western edge as 840 miles long. Divide that in half and you end up pretty close to the spot which the Spanish christened Big South. Individual assumptions aside, the North Coast begins at Big Sur.

Even without the mathematics, it is a logical choice. Big Sur is the southern boundary of the coast redwood, a conifer which as everyone knows grows naturally only along California's northern coastline. Here, stretching northward for hundreds of miles (but seldom more than 20 miles inland), is the world's legacy of tall trees—ancient sentinels whose ancestors once forested much of the earth. Their California history goes back 20 million years. Their beginnings predate the dinosaurs.

Exactly when or where the first redwoods pushed toward the sun is uncertain, though fossil records indicate the giant trees have existed for at least 160 million years. It was a prolific family that grew to encompass several species, and at its zenith its empire reached across Western Europe, Asia, Iceland, Greenland, and most of North America. But then the earth pushed upward and the ice moved down. And when at last the land stood fast and the creeping chill subsided, most of the giant trees were gone.

Most. But not all. Three redwood cousins survive. And while all claim similar characteristics, each has a fingerprint as individual as those of human relatives. The smallest is *Metasequoia glyptostroboides*, or dawn redwood, a deciduous species that lives naturally only in a remote section of China where it seldom grows higher than 140 feet or exceeds a diameter of six feet. The *Sequoiadendron giganteum*, or giant sequoia, is the goliath of California's Sierra Nevada, living in an oft-frozen realm and averaging heights of 280 feet, diameters up to 35 feet, and years that span 3,600.

By contrast, the *Sequoia sempervirens*, or coast redwood, lives only along California's northwestern edge where winters are mild, precipitation averages 80 to 100 inches annually, and fog smothers the land in any season. In such an atmosphere the coastal cousin reaches heights in excess of 300 feet, diameters up to 22 feet, and a lifespan of 2,200 years. It is the legendary giant of the plant world. And the king of them all resides just south of the Oregon border, deep within the primeval reaches of Redwood National Park. Here, on the broad, alluvial flats of the serpentine Redwood Creek stands the world's tallest living thing—a nearly 370-foot-high patriarch whose feathery crown rules over a kingdom of flickering light and shade, fog-filled spaces, and a palpable silence.

If the paths into the coast redwoods are well worn, those into the wine lands of the Napa and Sonoma Valleys are entrenched as deeply as the Oregon Trail on the Nebraska prairie. Easy to see why. This has been the heart of the California wine district since the early 1800s when the padres at the Sonoma mission, needing a source for their altar wines, planted the first vineyard north of San Francisco. Perhaps they took special care with their watering and pruning. Maybe they prayed for just the right number of warm, sunny days and cool evenings. Or maybe they were, after all, just lucky. Whatever the circumstance, the padres' vineyard flourished, each year producing quantities of fat, juicy grapes that fermented into fine wines.

Hard to keep something like that a secret. And, like all good things worth knowing, word got around. By the time Mexico secularized the church holdings in the 1830s, the vineyard was already noteworthy, and who more likely to designate himself the new owner than General Mariano Vallejo, the Mexican governor appointed to administer all church holdings in the north. But he wasn't alone for long. By the 1840s a smattering of other privately-owned vineyards dotted the two valleys, and by the 1850s many of the European immigrants who had failed to find their fortune in the Sierran gold fields returned to the San Francisco area to do the one thing they knew best—winemaking.

Almost by accident a new industry was born. Between 1860 and 1880 long, straight rows of vines stretched ever further across the fertile flats and up the sides of the narrow ridge that separated the two valleys, and wine cellars and hop barns soon rose above the legion of green like great, stone castles transplanted from some European countryside. By 1890 the relatively young vineyards were producing 25 million gallons of wine annually, and so fine was its composition that nearly half of the California wines entered in the 1890 Paris Exposition earned gold medals.

By 1919, the Golden State had become America's leading wine producer, and although the Prohibition years of 1920 to 1933 put more than a few crinks in the fledgling industry, the spunky California vintners picked themselves up, literally from ruins, and with a rare mixture of science and art, quietly started over. Their plan was simple: produce premium wines that did not require consumer indebtedness in order to pay for them. Excellent quality and fair prices would once again make the Golden State America's leading wine producer. And so it was. In 1941 the wine lands produced 89 million gallons of wine; in 1960, 129 million gallons; and in 1984, 375 million gallons. The industry had been reborn—and California wines were well on their way to becoming legends in their own time.

Today, nearly two million people annually visit the more than 250 Napa and Sonoma wineries to observe first-hand how wine is grown, harvested, crushed, fermented, and bottled. Guided tours through pungent cellars crowded with redwood and oak cooperage is the usual plan of the day, along with as many tasting-room stop-offs as can reasonably be accommodated. But there is more to the wine land than a sip of Riesling here and a Cabernet Sauvignon there. This is an area rich in history—and those willing to wend their way through Sonoma's crowded streets can see for themselves the place where it all began. It is a small plot of land called State Historic Landmark Number 739. But it is actually the padres' vineyard, and those with imaginations as fertile as the Sonora soil claim the brown-cassocked friars still walk amongst the vines.

It has been said that there are actually two Californias, and if one compares the conifered ramps of the north with the palm-treed flats of the south, it seems an obvious declaration. And even though the Golden State's southern sector boasts the sugar-coated likes of Hollywood and Disneyland, it is the northern reaches that claim the greatest diversity and all-around natural beauty. It is timely while it is timeless. How, you might inquire, can I make such seemingly opinionated statements? Simple. Ask the multiplied millions of Southlanders where they go to get away from it all. Our answers will be Big Sur. Carmel. Monterey. The Sierra. Lassen National Park. The Sacramento Delta. San Francisco. Lake Shasta. The Redwoods. All in Northern California. Right?

Sandra L. Keith
San Diego

1 Pigeon Point Lighthouse is perhaps the most spectacular of the many lighthouses that guard Northern California's jagged coastline. At a height of 115 feet, this giant masonry structure has been altered little since its completion in 1872.

2 The Siskiyou Mountains, in the
northwest corner of the state, are a
botanically diverse range. Many endemic
plants, such as the *Siskiyou lewisia*, flourish
in these rugged mountains.

3 El Capitan and Half Dome in Yosemite National Park shine in the final moments of sunset as an early autumn storm clears.

4 The recently restored Mission San José, originally built in 1797, is one of the 21 missions erected in the late 18th century by Father Junípero Serra.

5 (*right*) Pinnacles National Monument contains the only complete example of Coast Range chapparral in the National Park System. The weathered rocks, remnants of an ancient volcano, can be viewed along the crest of the High Peaks Trail.

6 Confined to the foggy regions, California's coast redwoods survive in a 450-mile-long stretch of coast that extends from the Santa Lucia Mountains north to just above the Oregon border. Hiking and camping are available in Del Norte Coast Redwoods State Park, at the northern end of the redwood region.

7 (*right*) Scenic Coast Highway 1 through Big Sur, completed in 1937, clings precariously to one of California's most dramatic coastlines.

8 Fort Ross was the north-coast outpost for Russian fur traders in the 19th century. The original fort was built in 1812, and the small wooden chapel was finished around 1824. After repeated changes due to earthquake and fire, the chapel was restored to its present state in 1974.

9 (*right*) The Golden Gate Bridge, viewed here from Baker Beach in Golden Gate National Recreation Area, was completed in 1937 and spans the mile-wide mouth of San Francisco Bay.

10 Western azalea grows in moist, open areas near the coast. The large flowers bloom from May to June, filling the air with their sweet fragrance.

11 (*right*) Drakes Beach in Point Reyes National Seashore is named in honor of Sir Francis Drake, who allegedly careened his ship, the *Golden Hind*, here in June, 1597.

12 California's capital was moved several times, all in Northern California locations, before it was finally settled in Sacramento, in the heart of the great Central Valley.

13 (*right*) The Minarets tower over Ediza Lake in the heart of the Ansel Adams Wilderness in the Sierra Nevada. This wilderness, formerly called Minarets, was renamed for Adams, a native California photographer and conservationist, after his death in 1984.

14 Wild mustard adds color to vineyards in the Napa Valley each winter.

15 The Hope Kiln Winery in the Russian River region of Sonoma County is evidence that wine is a major industry throughout Northern California.

16 Quaking aspen—the name refers to the leaves, which flutter with the slightest breeze. Deer and elk browse the twigs and foliage. Beavers, rabbits and other mammals eat the bark and buds.

17 (*right*) One of the major attractions of Monterey's 17-Mile Drive is The Lone Cypress.

18 Autumn color sweeps the vineyards each October and November, bringing a bright and festive end to the harvest season in the Valley of the Moon of Sonoma County.

19 (*right*) The Huntington mill and ore crusher in Plumas-Eureka State Park are relics of mining operations that began with the discovery of gold on Eureka Peak in 1851.

20 (*left*) The winter-whited foothills of the Sierra Nevada's eastern escarpment loom above the Owens Valley near Big Pine.

21 Yellow bush lupines bloom on the headlands above Stump Beach Cove in Salt Point State Park.

22 Winter reflections of El Capitan,
Yosemite National Park.

23 Old Sacramento State Historic Park was once a bustling 19th-century transportation center. The area is still a center of activity, complete with restored and reconstructed Gold Rush buildings and a railroad museum.

24 The California Tree—in Grant Grove of Sequoia National Park—is thought to be one of the loveliest *Sequoiadendron giganteum*, or Big Trees. It is remarkably free of fire scars, and although a 1967 fire burned 25 feet off its top, the California Tree still stands about 255 feet high and bears a 30 foot diameter.

25 (*right*) The sea continually shapes and reshapes the coastline, creating a sawtoothed shore where wind-whipped waves chew up rocky headlands, pummel boulders into cobbles, and sculpt arches that eventually collapse—leaving tiny islets as ghostly reminders of land's former edge.

26 (*left*) A variety of oaks dominate the lowland valleys and foothills of California.

27 The huge tailing wheels of the Kennedy Mine in Jackson were built in 1912 to carry waste gravels away from the mine. The Kennedy Mine claimed some of the deepest vertical shafts in the world, extending over 5,000 feet into the ground. Today, only two of the original four wheels remain.

28 (*left*) Mt. Shasta, at 14,162 feet in elevation, is composed of two volcanic cones: Shasta and Shastina. Shastina, a small cone that rises from the western flank is one and a half miles west of the main summit and stands 12,300 feet high.

29 Jagged sea stacks, headlands and an emerald ocean are the trademark of the Big Sur coast. Here, at the mouth of Palo Colorado Canyon, where ocean beats against the land, the ocean is victor.

30 (*left*) Jeffery Pines and quaking aspens line the course of Convict Creek as it tumbles towards the Owens Valley below Mt. Morrison.

31 Douglas iris and wooley *lasthenia* at the mouth of the Gualala River, Gualala Point County Park.

32 (*left*) The Bidwell Mansion in Chico was the home of pioneer ranchers John and Annie Bidwell. It is now preserved as the Bidwell Mansion State Historic Park.

33 The symmetrical colonnades of Devil's Postpile vary in shape—some have four sides, others as many as seven. An easy trail winds to the top and affords close-up views of the mosaic-tile-like design chiseled by long-forgotten glaciers.

34 Lake Tahoe is 22 miles long and 8-12 miles wide. The 71-mile-long road around the lake offers excellent views. The name, Tahoe, is thought to be derived from a Washo Indian word meaning "big water." Lake Tahoe is 1,600 feet deep at an altitude of 6,229 feet.

35 (*right*) Mt. Lassen, the southernmost of the Cascade volcanoes, reflects in the placid waters of Manzanita Lake in Lassen Volcanic National Park.

36 (*left*) Though Redwood National Park was created to protect the last remaining virgin coast redwoods, it also contains some of California's wildest coastline. This view is north from Split Rock.

37 The Sierra Buttes are the heart of one of the most popular recreation areas of the northern Sierra; numerous lakes, such as Sand Lake, offer fishing, swimming and boating.

38 Fully half of Point Lobos State Reserve is underwater, and it is considered to be one of the richest aquatic habitats in California. It is a popular scuba-diving spot and the many coves, like China Cove, harbor the endangered California sea otter.

39 The Monterey Bay Pier has been the center of activity for the
Monterey fishing industry since its inception more than 100 years ago.

40 (*left*) Devil's Postpile National Monument sits between Yosemite and Kings Canyon National Parks in the Sierra Nevada. The Monument claims Devil's Postpile, an ancient lava flow remnant that, over the eons, has been exposed, fractured and eroded into a hodgepodge of basalt columns that resemble the pipes of a giant organ.

41 The John Muir Trail, Northern California's most popular, begins at Yosemite Valley and ends at Whitney Portal. Where it crosses Island Pass in the Ansel Adams Wilderness, Banner Peak and Mt. Ritter come into view.

42 Burney Creek wells up from a subterranean source and divides into two fairly equal flows of water to form Burney Falls. McArthur-Burney Falls State Park sits midway between Mount Lassen and Shasta.

43 (*right*) Covered bridges are uncommon in California. This one over the Stanislaus River at Knights Ferry (Sierra Nevada foothills) is even more unusual because of its length.

44 (*left*) The town of Mendocino, famous as an art community, is surrounded by Mendocino Headlands State Park.

45 Whether it is considered a large shrub or a small tree, the western redbud's cloud of pink blooms make it one of the showiest specimens of the state's canyons, foothills, and mountains.

46 Schonchin Butte, a large cinder cone, stands guard over the winter landscape of Lava Beds National Monument. Though established to protect a variety of features, the lava tube caves are the major attraction. Nineteen of them are open for exploration by the public.

47 The clear, blue waters of Lake Tahoe make this popular resort area a recreational paradise. Boating, fishing and waterskiing can occupy the summer visitor's day.

48 The Grand Sentinel towers over the Kings River in Kings Canyon National Park.

49 (*right*) The U.S. Weather Bureau cites Point Reyes as the foggiest, windiest station—bar none—between Canada and Mexico. Point Reyes was declared a National Seashore in 1963. It contains 64,000 acres.

50 (*left*) The Great Beach sweeps along an eleven-mile, unbroken stretch of beach and breakers in Point Reyes National Seashore.

51 The northeast boundary of Yosemite National Park is etched along the summit of Sawtooth Ridge, a prominent feature that can be seen from Bridgeport Valley.

52 The rhododendrons are the stars of the summer flower display in the coastal redwood forest in Redwood National Park. During late May and lasting through June, these magnificent blooms light up the ridgelines with their bright pink flowers.

53 (*right*) The waxy leaves and flowers of the yellow pond-lily glisten in the early morning light at Lagoon Creek in Redwood National Park.

54 (*left*) The spectacular tufa formations of Mono Lake are visible now because of decades of water diversions. Today, environmentalists battle to restore the water flow to levels that will guarantee that this important bird rookery will remain productive.

55 Most of Yosemite National Park is Federally Designated Wilderness, and over 700 miles of trails lace the backcountry. Here, sunset reflects off an alpine tarn in the Cathedral Lakes Basin.

56 Bodega Bay is one of the many centres of commercial fishing activity on the north coast.

57 (*right*) The Leesville Road winds its way through the Coast Range of Colusa County towards the Sacramento Valley.

58 (*left*) Rose-covered shack near Fort Bragg.

59 Brokeoff Mountain and Mt. Diller, seen here with red heather, are the largest remnants of a giant volcano. This volcano, often called Mt. Tehama, once dominated the southern part of what is now Lassen Volcanic National Park.

60 (*left*) Heavy snows can come as early as October in the Hoover Wilderness. Quaking aspens and Gabbro Peak in the Sierra Nevada show the evidence.

61 Bumpass Hell is Lassen's most famous thermal valley. Even in winter, under 20 feet of snow, the thermal features operate at full blast, heated by underground pools and rivulets of magma.

62 (*left*) The Napa Valley is the prime wine-producing region of California—and for good reason. Mild winters, abundant rains and plenty of sunshine provide the ideal climate for growing premium-quality grapes.

63 El Capitan is the world's largest exposed block of solid granite. The Spaniards named it "The Chief"—an apt title. The titan's sleek, unbroken profile rises 3,569 feet above the floor of Yosemite Valley.

64 Tenaya and hundreds of other lakes scattered throughout the Sierra Nevada reveal the pathways of ancient glaciers that once covered the high country of Yosemite National Park.

65 (*right*) The ghost town of Bodie is now maintained in a state of "arrested deterioration," though many of the buildings have been restored. What remains today is only a fraction of the original Gold Rush period town—a fire in 1932 destroyed most of the buildings.

66 The intertidal estuary at the mouth of the Klamath River is the beginning of some of the best steelhead and salmon fishing in Northern California. From mid-July, when the king salmon enter, until September, when the steelhead begin their spawning runs, anglers toss many varieties of lures, bait and artificial flies to try for a chance to catch a "big one."

67 (*right*) In time this arch on the Santa Cruz coastline will be worn down, creating but another offshore isle.

68 On the eastern escarpment of the Sierra Nevada, aspens follow the winding watercourse of Laurel Creek on its journey to the Owens River Valley below.

69 (right) Though its distance from California's most active fault, the San Andreas, can be measured in feet instead of miles, the mission at San Juan Bautista (1797) still stands on the edge of the peaceful town.

70 (*left*) Aspens show color along Monument Ridge, as seen from upper Summer Meadows in Toiyabe National Forest.

71 While tracking a grizzly bear near Murphys in the spring of 1852, A.T. Dowd came upon a grove of giant, red trees. He had stumbled into what is now Calaveras Big Trees State Park, and brought the world's attention to the Sierra redwoods.

72 (*left*) The Trinidad Memorial Lighthouse, dedicated to fishermen lost at sea, stands over Trinidad Bay—one of the most popular ocean sport-fishing areas in the state.

73 Poppies, the California state flower, bloom in profusion from the coast to the Sierra foothills. They reach their peak of bloom in May, and are seen here with slender *clarkia*.

74 Hot Creek, a tributary of the Owens River, is a favorite natural hot springs area—in both summer and winter.

75 (*right*) Conway Summit (8,138 feet) is the highest point on U.S. Highway 395. This major north/south artery travels the entire length of the eastern Sierra on its way from Canada to Mexico.

76 (*left*) James Marshall's discovery of gold in 1848 at this site north of Placerville was an event that changed California's history. Today, at Marshall Gold Discovery Site, the ore wagons are still and the 49ers are gone—but the legacy of life in the gold fields lives on.

77 Mono County's Bridgeport Courthouse, the second oldest in California, was built on a granite foundation brought from Bodie, a Gold Rush town 20 miles to the east.

78 Yosemite Falls, highest in North America, is the second highest in the world. The 2,425 foot waterfall is cast in three phases. The upper falls drop 1,430 feet; the middle cascades are one quarter mile long; the lower falls, pictured here, drop 320 feet.

79 (*right*) McWay Creek makes its final fall into McWay Cove on the Big Sur Coast at Julia Pfeiffer Burns State Park.

80 Headlands, culminating at Pfeiffer Point, plunge into the ocean on the Big Sur Coast.

81 (*right*) Emerald Bay, the jewel of Lake Tahoe, was formed by a moraine left behind by glaciers that once flowed down from the Sierra crest.

82 About 75 groves of Sierra redwoods inhabit a 260-mile-long strip in the Sierra Nevada; the largest concentration of them is in Sequoia and Kings Canyon National Parks. Here they attain their largest size.

83 (*right*) Half Dome, North Dome and The Washington Column rise above Stoneman Meadow in Yosemite National Park.

84 The view from the top of Morro Rock in Sequoia National Park is worth the 300-foot vertical climb. From the top, one can see the Great Western Divide to the east and the San Joaquin Valley to the west.

85 (*right*) Shore pine are silhouetted against a winter sunset at Salt Point State Park.

86 (*overleaf*) The sun sets over Trinidad, on Northern California's coast.